I0395556

ONE HUNDRED

Horse Doodles

AND 100 FACTS ABOUT HORSES

LOREM
IPSUM

Published in 2020 by Universum Publishing.

Copyright ©2020 i-can-draw-a-horse.com

Cover art and illustrations by i-can-draw-a-horse.com
Design & typesetting by vava.lv
©2020 vava.lv

All rights reserved.
No part of this publication may be reproduced, stored in a retrieval system, or transmitted in any form or by any means, electronic, mechanical, photocopying, recording or otherwise, without the prior permission of the copyright owner

ISBN 978-1-9114180-0-9 (paperback)

2020

FACT 1

HORSES HAVE A HEAD

FACT 2

AND TWO EYES ON IT

FACT 3

HORSES HAVE ALMOST 360 DEGREE OF VISION

FACT 4

THEY HAVE BIGGER EYES THAN ANY OTHER MAMMAL THAT LIVES ON LAND

FACT 5

HORSES CAN SEE BETTER AT NIGHT THAN YOU, HUMANS

FACT 6

HORSES' EYES ARE THE SAME SIZE AT BIRTH AS WHEN THEY ARE FULLY GROWN

Fact 7

HORSES SHOW EMOTIONS WITH THEIR EYES

Fact 8

AND WITH THEIR EARS TOO

FACT 9

BOTH EARS, OF COURSE

Fact **10**

EARS ARE VERY IMPORTANT

Fact 11

A LOT OF COMMUNICATION BETWEEN HORSES GOES THROUGH THEM

Fact **12**

EACH EAR CAN ROTATE UP TO 180 DEGREES

Fact **13**

THIS PROVIDES THEM WITH A POTENTIAL FOR 360 DEGREES OF HEARING WITHOUT HAVING TO MOVE THEIR HEAD

Fact **14**

ALSO THEY USE NOSTRILS TO SHOW THEIR EMOTIONS

Fact **15**

BOTH OF THOSE, TOO

Fact 16

HORSES CAN'T BREATHE THROUGH THEIR MOUTH

Fact **17**

REMEMBER: EYES, EARS AND NOSTRILS ARE USED TO SHOW A MOOD

Fact **18**

HORSES HAVE A NECK

Fact 19

ON THE NECK THEY HAVE A MANE

Fact **20**

IT'S LIKE HUMAN HAIR

Fact **21**

MANE GROWS FROM THE TOP OF THE NECK

Fact 22

AND REACHING FROM THE POLL TO THE WITHERS

Fact **23**

MANE INCLUDES THE FORELOCK

Fact 24

AND IT'S SOOO SWEET

Fact **25**

PONIES USUALLY HAVE THE THICKEST MANES

Fact 26

YES, PONIES ARE HORSES TOO

Fact 27

OK, HORSES ALSO HAVE FOUR LEGS

Fact 28

TWO FRONT AND TWO BACK

Fact 29

AND TWO LEFT AND TWO RIGHT

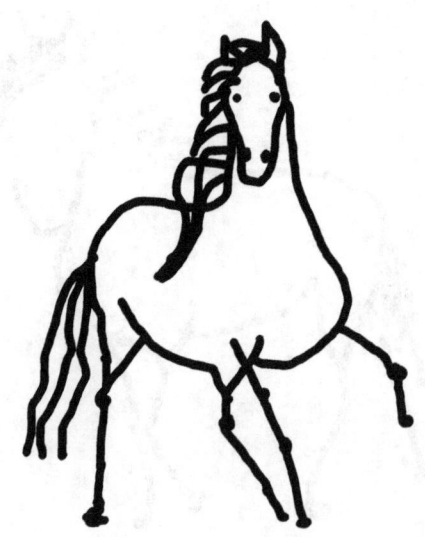

Fact **30**

BUT STILL FOUR OF THEM

Fact **31**

EACH LEG ENDS WITH A HOOF

Fact **32**

THE HOOF IS MADE FROM THE SAME MATERIAL AS YOUR NAILS

Fact *33*

THE HOOF HAS A FROG

Fact **34**

NOT A REAL FROG, BUT A PART OF THE HOOF CALLED 'FROG'

Fact 35

HORSES EAT GRASS, THEY ARE GRAZING ANIMALS

Fact **36**

LIKE HUMANS, HORSES HAVE LIFE STAGES

Fact 37

FOAL – UP TO ONE YEAR

Fact **38**

YEARLING – BETWEEN ONE AND TWO YEARS OLD

Fact 39

COLT – A BOY UP TO FOUR YEARS OLD

Fact 40

FILLY - A GIRL UP TO FOUR YEARS OLD

Fact 41

STALLION AND MARE – AFTER FOUR YEARS OLD

Fact 42

HORSES ARE NATURALLY CURIOUS

Fact **43**

AND APT TO INVESTIGATE THINGS THEY HAVE NOT SEEN BEFORE

Fact 44

THEY ARE VERY SMART

Fact **45**

HORSES KNOW THE DIFFERENCE BETWEEN 'MORE AND LESS'

Fact **46**

HORSES SLEEP STANDING UP

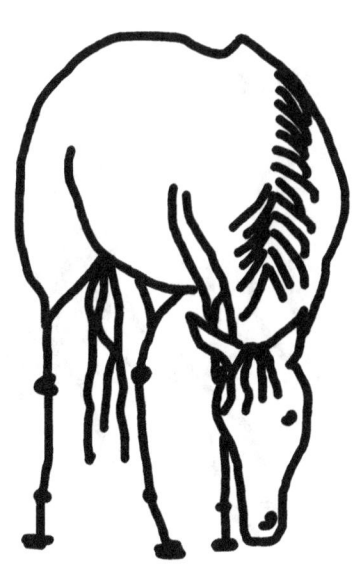

Fact 47

OR LYING DOWN

Fact 48

AND THEY SLEEP IN A LOT OF SHORT PERIODS

Fact **49**

ABOUT FIFTEEN MINUTES EACH PERIOD

Fact **50**

NOT IN ONE GO

Fact 51

AND IN TOTAL CLOSE TO THREE HOURS PER A DAY

Fact 52

THEY MAY BE BORED IN THE STABLE

Fact **53**

AND MAY START TO PLAY PRANKS

Fact **54**

LIKE OPEN THEIR PADDOCK

Fact 55

AND FREE THEIR FRIENDS

Fact **56**

HORSES ARE HIGHLY SOCIAL ANIMALS

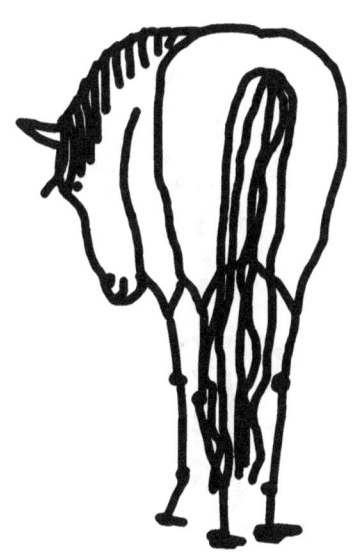

Fact 57

HORSES LOVE BEING AMONG OTHERS OF THEIR OWN KIND

Fact **58**

THEY WILL GET LONELY IF KEPT ALONE

Fact 59

WILD HORSES TYPICALLY LIVE IN GROUPS OF 3-20 HORSES

Fact 60

GROUPS USUALLY CONSIST OF ONE STALLION, SEVERAL MARES, AND THEIR OFFSPRING

Fact **61**

AMONG THE MARES, ONE EMERGES AS THE LEAD MARE

Fact **62**

SHE DECIDES WHEN THE HERD WILL GRAZE, DRINK, SLEEP AND WHERE THEY WILL TRAVEL

Fact **63**

HORSES WERE DOMESTICATED OVER FIVE THOUSAND YEARS AGO

Fact 64

THEY HELPED US EVOLVE INTO WHAT WE ARE

Fact **65**

HORSES HELP US PLOW

Fact 66

MOVE LOADS

Fact 67

THEY LET US RIDE ON THEIR BACKS

Fact **68**

AND CARRY US IN CARRIAGES

Fact **69**

HA, BUT NOW WE CARRY THEM!

Fact **70**

HORSES HAVE A TAIL

Fact 71

AND IT'S BEAUTIFUL

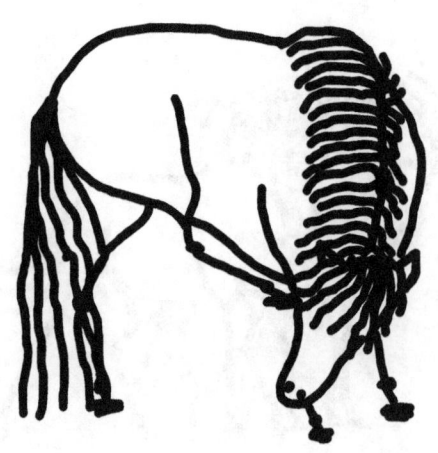

Fact 72

BUT IT IS ALSO
VERY IMPORTANT FOR HORSES

Fact *73*

AND UNIQUE

Fact 74

AND VERY SHORT

Fact 75

BUT HAS LONG HAIR ON IT

Fact 76

ITS MAIN PURPOSE IS TO PREVENT HEAT LOSS

Fact *77*

THAT IS WHY A ZEBRA'S TAIL IS LONGER AND HAS FEW HAIR

Fact 78

YEAH, IT'S COLD HERE IN WINTER

Fact 79

THE TAIL IS ALSO USED TO REPEL INSECTS

Fact **80**

HAVE YOU SEEN HORSES STANDING WITH ONE'S HEAD NEXT TO THE OTHER TAIL?

Fact **81**

THEY ARE KEEPING FLIES OFF EACH OTHER'S FACES!

Fact 82

ALSO THE TAIL IS USED IN THEIR BODY LANGUAGE

Fact **83**

A FLATTENED TAIL MAY MEAN FEAR (UNLESS IT'S COLD)

Fact **84**

A TAIL LIFTED OVER THE BACK INDICATES ENTHUSIASM

Fact 85

A SWISHING TAIL MAY BE SWATTING AT A FLY, OR IT MAY BE EXPRESSING IRRITATION

Fact 86

A HORSE WILL HOLD ITS TAIL TENSELY OR EVEN CROOKED IF ITS UNHAPPY

Fact 87

OR IT FEELS PAIN

Fact **88**

A SWISHED TAIL COMBINED WITH PINNED EARS IS A CLEAR WARNING OF FORTHCOMING AGGRESSION

Fact **89**

BETTER NOT GET TOO CLOSE

Fact **90**

PEOPLE CAN MAKE BOWS FROM HORSE TAIL HAIR

Fact 91

NOT FOR ARCHERY

Fact 92

BUT FOR PLAYING MUSIC

Fact **93**

HORSE HAIR IS ALSO USED FOR UPHOLSTERY

Fact 94

IN HARD-WEARING FABRIC CALLED HAIRCLOTH

Fact **95**

YOU CAN FIND JEWELRY MADE OUT OF HORSE HAIR

Fact 96

AND PAINT BRUSHES FOR ARTISTS

Fact 97

OR BRUSHES FOR ANY OTHER PURPOSES

Fact **98**

AND LONG TIME AGO IT WAS USED FOR FISHING LINES

Fact 99

HUNDREDS OF YEARS AGO SURGEONS USED HORSEHAIR TO SUTURE

Fact 100

OMG THEY ARE BEAUTIFUL, AREN'T THEY?

DO YOU LOVE ZEBRAS AS WELL?

YOU CAN FIND MORE XORSE DRAWINGS ON THE WWW.I-CAN-DRAW-A-HORSE.COM

www.ingramcontent.com/pod-product-compliance
Lightning Source LLC
Chambersburg PA
CBHW081337080526
44588CB00017B/2655